We Love
you
Always!

Presented To

Mark Robert

From

Uncle Scott & Aunt Lisa

On the Occasion of

Your Baptism

Jesus In Pictures for Little Eyes

Jesus
In Pictures
for Little Eyes

Kenneth N. Taylor

Illustrated by Annabel Spenceley

MOODY PUBLISHERS
CHICAGO

First published in the USA
by Moody Publishers, Chicago

Worldwide co-edition organized and
produced by Angus Hudson Ltd,
Concorde House, Grenville Place,
Mill Hill, London NW7 3SA, England
Tel: +44 20 8959 3668
Fax: +44 20 8959 3678
e-mail: coed@angushudson.com

ISBN 0-8024-3059-7

1 2 3 4 5 6 07 06 05 04 03
Printed in China

Contents

Angels Tell
of Jesus' Birth

IT IS NIGHTTIME, and these men
are out in the fields taking care of
their sheep. Can you see their
sheep? But now what is happening?
Who are these angels who have
come? They are telling these men
that God's Son has been born.
He is a little baby. The
angels are glad and
the men are glad.

Luke 2:1-15

**What are the angels
telling the men?**

Shepherds Visit Baby Jesus

THE MEN who were taking care of the sheep have come to find God's Son. The angels told them where to find Him, and now they have come to see the baby Jesus. There is the baby and His mother. The mother's name is Mary. God is the baby's Father.

Luke 2:16-18

Who is this baby?

Wise Men Follow the Star

WHO ARE THESE MEN? They are riding on camels. Where are the men going in such a hurry? They are going to find God's Son. They are bringing many gifts to give Him. They know where to go because God has sent a star for them to follow. The star will take them to the baby Jesus.

Matthew 2:1-9

Where are the men going?

Wise Men Give Their Gifts

THE MEN who were on the camels have come a long way. Now they have found the little baby they were looking for. They know that the baby is God's Son. They have brought many gifts to give Him. They are holding them out for Him to see while they worship Him and thank God.

Matthew 2:10,11

Are the men giving presents to baby Jesus?

Simeon Holds Baby Jesus

CAN YOU SEE the old man who is holding the baby? He has waited all his life to see God's baby Son. He has never been so happy in all his life before, because now at last Jesus is born and he can hold Him in his arms. He knows that Jesus will take care of God's people.

Luke 2:25-38

Why is the man so happy?

Jesus Visits the Temple

THIS IS another picture of Jesus. He has become an older boy now. These men are preachers and teachers. The boy Jesus is asking them questions. These men cannot understand how a boy can know so much about God. They do not know that this boy is God's Son. This is Jesus.

Luke 2:40-52

Why does Jesus know so much about God?

John Baptizes Jesus

NOW JESUS is a man. Another man whose name is John is pointing up to God and praying. John will baptize Jesus. As soon as Jesus is baptized, He will hear God saying, "This is my Son and I love Him. Listen to what He tells you to do." God wants everyone to know that this is His Son.

Matthew 3:13-17

What will God say?

Jesus Says 'No' to Satan

JESUS HAS gone far away. He is alone. He has not eaten anything for breakfast, or lunch, or supper. He has not eaten anything for forty days. Soon Satan, God's enemy, will come and try to get Jesus to do something bad, but Jesus will not listen to bad Satan. Jesus is God's Son, and He is good. Jesus does only what God says.

Matthew 4:1-11

Will Jesus ever do anything bad?

Jesus Chooses His Helpers

JESUS ASKS twelve men to be His special friends. These men are called His disciples. They go with Jesus wherever He goes and help Him in all His work. They are happy to help Him. Some of the names of these men are Peter, John, James, Thomas, and Andrew. These twelve men are Jesus' helpers.

Mark 3:13-19

Who are these men?

Jesus Changes Water to Wine

ONE DAY Jesus was at a wedding. The people eating dinner needed more wine to drink. Jesus told the servants to fill up six big jars with water. And do you know what? It wasn't water anymore. It was better wine than they had ever tasted. Jesus can do things like that because He is God.

John 2:1-11

Can Jesus help us when we need Him?

Men Buy and Sell in God's House

JESUS IS making some men get out of God's house. They didn't come to love God and pray. No, they are doing things there that God does not want them to do. They are selling things to get a lot of money and be rich. Jesus says that they are in His Father's house and they must not do things like that when they are there.

John 2:13-17

What does Jesus want these men to do?

Peter Catches Many Fish

DO YOU SEE Jesus standing there? He told Peter to throw his fishing net in the water. Peter did not think that there would be any fish, but he did what Jesus told him, and now just see how many fish there are! Peter obeyed Jesus, and now Peter has all these fish. Can you see all the fish? There are almost too many to count.

Luke 5:1-11

Why did all these fish come into the net?

Men Bring a Sick Friend to Jesus

LOOK AT the men at the top of the picture. They brought their friend to Jesus. They took away part of the roof and lowered him down through the roof, right in front of Jesus. The man could not walk. Jesus told the man to get well, and now he is getting up. Jesus made him well right away.

Luke 5:17-26

How did the men get their friend down to Jesus?

Nicodemus Talks to Jesus

IT IS NIGHTTIME, and Jesus is talking to a man named Nicodemus. Jesus is telling him how to get to heaven. He says, "Nicodemus, you cannot get there by yourself, but God will take you there if you believe in Me. God loves you, Nicodemus." Jesus died so that Nicodemus could go to heaven. Jesus died so that you and I can go to heaven if we love Him.

John 3:1-5, 14-18

Why did Jesus die?

A Little Boy
Is Well Again

YESTERDAY THIS little boy was
so sick that he didn't want to
run and play. His father was
sad. He went to see Jesus.
He asked Jesus to come
and make the little boy
well. Jesus told the father
to go home and the little
boy would be all right.
Jesus is far away, but
He makes the little boy
well again.

John 4:46-54

Is the little boy sick now?

Jesus Teaches the People

JESUS IS talking to the people. They want to hear what Jesus says. Some of these people will love Jesus always, and some will go away and not want Him to be their Friend anymore. If Jesus is not their Friend, then God will not let them come to heaven. Jesus wants to be your Friend too. If you want Him to be your Friend, tell Him so now.

Matthew 5:1-11

Is Jesus your Friend?

Two Men
Build Houses

JESUS TOLD a story about two men. One of them built his house on the sand. He was a foolish man. It rained and rained, and all of the sand washed away, and the house fell down. The other man built his house on a rock. Even though it rains and rains, the rock and the house will not wash away. He is a wise man.

Matthew 7:24-29

Will the house on the rock fall down?

42

Jesus Makes a Dead Man Live

JESUS IS helping a man sit up.
The man was dead, and his
mother was sad. Jesus tells him
to be alive again. When Jesus
says that, all of a sudden the
man begins to move. He opens his
eyes and sees Jesus, and he sees
his mother too. The man and his
mother are glad, and Jesus is
glad.

Luke 7:11-16

What did Jesus tell the man to do?

Jesus Stops a Storm

JESUS AND his friends are in a boat. There is a great storm. The wind is blowing. It is raining hard. The friends are afraid the ship will sink. Is Jesus afraid? No, He isn't. Jesus is holding up His hands, and now the storm is going away. Jesus tells the storm to stop and it does.

Matthew 8:23-27

Is Jesus afraid?

Jesus Makes a Dead Girl Live

THIS LITTLE GIRL is twelve years old. She was very sick. Her father asked Jesus to make his little girl well again. Jesus takes the girl's hand and says, "Get up, little girl." Right away she sits up and gets out of bed. The little girl had died, but Jesus brought her back to life. That is why her mother and father are so surprised and happy.

Mark 5:22-43

Why are the mother and father so happy?

A Blind Man
Sees Again

JESUS IS talking here with a man who cannot see Him. The man is blind. Close your eyes now, and you can tell what it is like to be blind. Everything is dark. Someone told this man, "Jesus is coming!" The man cried out very loudly, "Jesus, please make my eyes well." Jesus touches his eyes and says, "Be open." And right away he can see.

Matthew 9:27-31

Could the man see Jesus?

A Man Is a Good Neighbor

THIS POOR man was going on a trip, and some bad men came and hurt him. They left him lying there on the road. Two men came walking along but didn't stop to help him. Then another man he didn't like came along and stopped. He is helping the poor man who is hurt. Jesus wants us to be kind to everyone, even people who hit us or don't like us.

Luke 10:30-37

Where is the man who is being kind?

52

Mary Listens to Jesus Teach

MARY IS sitting listening while Jesus talks to her. Do you see the other lady? Her name is Martha. She is Mary's sister. Martha is working very hard and wants Mary to help. But Jesus says, "No, let Mary sit here and listen, because that is even more important than getting supper." Jesus meant that we should always take time to talk to Him and listen to Him.

Luke 10:38-42

What does Jesus want Mary to do?

54

Jesus Talks with Bad Leaders

JESUS IS angry with these men. They say that they love God, but they really don't. They want to do things their own way instead of the way God says. They give money to God and go to God's house, but they do not love Him. Jesus wants them to love God. He does not want their money unless they love Him.

Luke 11:37-44

Do these men love God?

A Rich Farmer Forgets God

THIS MAN is a rich farmer. He has lots of money. But he does not love God. He has so much money and food that he doesn't know where to put it, so he is going to build a bigger barn. But tonight God will let this rich man die. He will not wake up tomorrow. The man is bad because he loves his farm but doesn't love God.

Luke 12:16-21

Does this man love God?

Jesus Teaches about God's Care

JESUS IS talking to His friends. He is telling them to look at the flowers. The flowers don't work hard to cook their suppers, do they? No, flowers don't need to work hard because God takes care of them. Jesus is telling His friends that God takes care of the flowers and He will take care of them too, if they ask Him, and if they do whatever He says.

Luke 12:27-32

Will God take care of you?

A Man Plants Seed

THIS MAN is planting seeds. He wants them to grow up into tall stalks of wheat. But look! The birds are eating up some of the seeds. Those seeds will not grow. Some of the seeds are falling down on the rocks and thorns. The seeds cannot grow there very well. But some of the seeds fall on good ground. They will grow up and become big plants.

Matthew 13:3-8

Where will the seeds grow best?

A Boy Shares His Bread and Fish

SEE HOW many people there are? They are all hungry. It is time to eat, and they don't have any food. One boy brought his lunch. The boy is giving his lunch to Jesus. Jesus will break the bread in pieces, and do you know what will happen? Jesus will make the five pieces of bread in the boy's lunch become enough bread for all the people to eat!

Matthew 14:15-23

What will Jesus do with the boy's lunch?

Jesus Walks on the Water

DO YOU SEE Jesus? He is walking on top of the water. Can you walk on top of water in your bathtub? No, of course not. But Jesus made the water. He can stand on it if He wants to. Peter is in the boat. He will step out on the water and walk toward Jesus. Then he will become frightened and begin to sink, and Jesus will come and save him.

Matthew 14:22-33

What will happen when Peter gets scared?

Jesus' Clothes Are Shiny

JESUS IS with Peter and James and John up on a high mountain. All of a sudden Jesus' clothes begin to shine and become brighter and brighter, and whiter than snow. Peter and James and John are frightened. Then they see two other men. Moses and Elijah have come down from heaven to talk to Jesus. Soon a bright cloud will come, and God's voice will say, "Jesus is My Son, listen to Him."

Matthew 17:1-9

What color did Jesus' clothes become?

Jesus Makes Lazarus Live

LAZARUS IS Jesus' friend. One day Lazarus got sick and died. His friends took his body and put it in the hole in the big rock. When Jesus came, He told the men to roll away the stone. Jesus prayed and asked God to make Lazarus alive. Now can you see what is happening? Lazarus is coming out again. He was dead but now he is alive.

John 11:1-45

Did Jesus make Lazarus alive?

Jesus Loves Children

JESUS LOVES little children. In this picture He is holding some of them on His lap and talking to them. Once Jesus' friends tried to send the children away. But Jesus wants the children to be with Him. He says, "Let the little children come to Me. Do not send them away, because I love them and want them with Me."

Matthew 19:13-15

Does Jesus love you?

Jesus Cries about a City

JESUS IS CRYING. He is looking at the city of Jerusalem. There are many people in this city. They do not love Jesus or His Father. Jesus knows that some day a great army will come and knock down their city. Jesus loves them and wants to help them, but they do not love Jesus, and that is why He is crying.

Luke 13:31-35

Why is Jesus crying?

A Shepherd Finds His Lost Sheep

THIS MAN lost one of his sheep. It ran away and fell down and couldn't get back up again. The man went to find it, and here he is picking it up. The man is good because he takes care of the sheep. Jesus is like that man. He wants to take care of us when we get lost. Jesus loves you very much. You can be one of His little lambs.

Luke 15:3-7

What is the man doing?

Perfume for Jesus

THIS WOMAN is putting perfume on Jesus' feet. The perfume cost a lot of money. The men sitting at the table with Jesus are telling Him that the lady shouldn't do this, but Jesus is glad. He wants her to do this because she is doing it to tell Jesus, "Thank You." Jesus has been kind to her. She has done many bad things, but Jesus will forgive her.

John 12:1-7

Can you tell Jesus, "Thank You," for what He has done for you?

A Boy Goes Away from Home

THIS YOUNG MAN is going away from home. His father doesn't want him to go. But the son thinks it will be more fun away from home. He asked his father to give him a lot of money, and now he will go away. Are you sorry that the boy is doing this? He should have stayed at home and helped his father instead of going away.

Luke 15:11-19

Does the young man want to stay home or go away?

A Boy Goes Back to His Father

HERE IS the young man who went away when his father didn't want him to. Now he has come back home. His father is very happy. After the son went away, he began to get very hungry, so he decided to come home again. He didn't know if his father would want him. But the father ran and welcomed him and is telling him how glad he is.

Luke 15:20-24

Is the father happy?

82

One Man
Thanks Jesus

DO YOU SEE the men walking away from Jesus? They were men with leprosy. That means they were so sick that everyone was afraid to go near them. When they saw Jesus, they called to Him and said, "Jesus, help us. Please help us." Jesus wanted to help, and He made all of them well. He healed them all, but only one man came back to tell Him, "Thank You."

Luke 17:11-19

Where is the man who is saying, "Thank You"?

Jesus Tells About Some Grape Growers

THIS MAN is lying here because he is dead. His father sent him to get the rent money from the people staying in his house. Instead they killed him. The father will punish these men because of the terrible thing they have done to his son. Jesus told this story because He is like the owner's son. People who don't love Him will lose the wonderful things that God, His Father, wants to give them.

Matthew 21:33-41

What will this man's father do?

A Poor Woman Gives to God

JESUS IS WATCHING the people in God's house. They are giving money to God. This woman has brought a few pennies. That is all she has, and she is giving it all to God. Jesus is glad she loves God so much. The rich men have put in lots more money, but they are still rich. The poor woman's few pennies are better than all the money from the rich people who don't love Him.

Mark 12:41-44

How much money does the woman have left?

Jesus Rides into the City

EVERYONE IS happy because Jesus has come to visit. All the people think Jesus has come to Jerusalem to be their king. See how some people are putting their coats on the ground and cutting down branches from the trees to make a path for Him. The people shout and thank God. They do not know that Jesus will soon be killed.

Matthew 21:1-11

What are the people putting down on the road?

Jesus Tells What Will Happen to Him

HERE IN this picture you can see Jesus talking to some of His friends. He is telling them about what will happen to Him. He is pointing up to heaven, telling them that soon He will go there to be with God, His Father. Jesus says that someday all His friends will come to heaven too, and live there with Him always.

Luke 22:14-22

Where is Jesus pointing?

A Great Dinner

THIS MAN has made a great dinner. He asked his rich friends to come, but they wouldn't. Then he invited the poor people who were sick and crippled and blind. Do you see them? They are glad to come and eat. The man is glad because of his new friends, but he is sorry because of those who would not come. Jesus wants you to come and live with Him someday.

Matthew 22:1-14

Does Jesus want you to come to Him?

Jesus Talks about Loving God

SOME MEN are asking Jesus about the most important rule to obey. Can you think what that rule would be? Would it be to eat nicely? Or would it be not going across the street alone? No. These things are important. But there is something even more important. Jesus says that the greatest thing to do is to love God. Do you love God? Do you do whatever He says?

Matthew 22:35-40

What are some things God wants you to do?

Jesus Eats His Last Supper

JESUS HAS a loaf of bread in His hand. He is breaking it into pieces for His disciples, who are eating supper with Him. Jesus is telling them that He must soon die. He died for you. He died for me. We have done bad things that God must punish. But God punished Jesus instead of us. Jesus didn't do anything bad, but God punished Him. Do you know why?

Luke 22:14-20

What is going to happen to Jesus?

Jesus Teaches about Heaven

JESUS IS telling His disciples what is going to happen. Some men are going to kill Him, but Jesus tells the disciples not to be afraid. Jesus will go away to His Father, up in heaven. When He gets there, He will get places ready for His disciples to come to live. He is getting a place ready for you to live in heaven too, if you love Jesus.

John 14:1-14

Where is Jesus now?

Jesus Prays in the Garden

JESUS IS praying all alone. He is talking to His Father in Heaven. Jesus is very, very sad. He knows that some men will take Him away and nail Him to a cross. He will die so that God will not need to punish you and me for the bad things we have done. Jesus does not want to die, but He will let the men kill Him. Jesus is glad to die for you.

Luke 22:39-48

Is Jesus happy or sad?

Judas Shows Where Jesus Is

DID YOU ever hear about a man named Judas Iscariot? Judas pretended that he was Jesus' friend. Some bad men said they would give Judas money if he would help them catch Jesus. Now Judas is bringing them to Jesus. It is night. Is Jesus going to run away? No, Jesus is standing, waiting. He could go away if He wanted to, but He will let them take Him.

Luke 22:47-54

Who is leading these bad people to Jesus?

Peter Tells a Lie

PETER IS one of Jesus' friends. He is getting warm by the fire with some of Jesus' enemies. The woman has asked Peter if Jesus is his Friend. He says that he doesn't know Jesus at all. Peter is telling a lie. He doesn't want the other people there to know he is Jesus' friend. Afterwards he will cry hard because he has done such a bad thing.

Matthew 26:69-75

What did Peter tell the girl?

Pilate Listens to the People

NOW THE PEOPLE have taken Jesus to Pilate. Pilate can let them kill Jesus or else let Jesus go. He thinks he ought to let Jesus go. He says Jesus hasn't done anything bad at all. See how angry the people are! They are shouting at Pilate, and Pilate is afraid of them. Soon he will give Jesus to the men so they can kill Him.

John 19:1-16

What do the people want Pilate to do?

Jesus Is Put on the Cross

THE BAD MEN have taken Jesus and have nailed His hands and His feet on these big pieces of wood so that He will die. Oh, what a terrible thing they are doing! Jesus was nailed there because He loves you and me. We have done bad things, and God should punish us. But God sent His dear Son, Jesus, to be punished for us. That is how much Jesus loves you. He died for you.

John 19:16-24

Does Jesus love you?

Jesus Is Dead

JESUS IS DEAD. His friends are putting His body into a great hole in the rock. They do not think they will ever see Jesus again. How sad they are! They do not know that soon He will become alive again and come out of the place where they are putting Him. God is going to bring Him back to life.

John 19:40-42

Will Jesus' body stay there in the hole?

Jesus Is Alive Again

THESE THREE women are Jesus' friends. They have come to His grave. But what is happening? An angel is inside where Jesus was. The angel tells them Jesus isn't there! Jesus is alive! He was dead, but God made Him alive again! Jesus said this would happen, but no one believed Him. Now His friends know that whatever Jesus says is always true. Aren't you glad that Jesus is alive?

Mark 16:1-8

What is the angel saying?

114

Jesus' Friends See Him

SOME OF Jesus' friends are meeting Him again. They thought Jesus was dead. They didn't know that Jesus was alive again. How surprised and happy they are! They know now that Jesus is God's Son, and they fall down at His feet and pray to Him. Jesus is saying, "Don't be afraid. Go and tell My other friends to go to the place where I told them to meet Me."

Matthew 28:8-11

Who are these women talking to?

Peter and John Run to the Grave

DO YOU see these two men running as fast as they can? One of them is Peter, and the other one is John. Why are they running so fast? The women have told them that Jesus is not in the grave but is alive again. Peter and John are going to see for themselves. What an exciting morning this was when Jesus came back to life again!

John 20:1-5

Where are the two men going?

The Grave
Is Empty

PETER AND JOHN ran right to the place where Jesus had been buried. Now Peter is inside, looking for Jesus. Is Jesus there? No, the cloth that was wrapped around Jesus is lying there, but Jesus has gone away. He is alive again. Peter is surprised. John is surprised too. Finally they know that Jesus is not dead anymore.

John 20:6-1

Where is Jesus?

Jesus Walks with Two Friends

THREE MEN are walking along a road. Two of them are going home. They are sad because they think Jesus is dead. The third man came along and is telling them more about Jesus and why He had to die. Later, the two men will realize that the third man is Jesus. They have been talking to Jesus and didn't know it!

Luke 24:13-32

Who is the third man?

Jesus Shows His Hands and Feet

THE DISCIPLES were talking together when suddenly Jesus was there. He didn't knock or come in the door. He was just there! He must have come right through the walls because Jesus can do anything. His disciples are scared, but Jesus says, "Don't be afraid, I am Jesus." He is showing them the holes in His hands and feet. Now they know it is really Jesus, who was nailed to the cross and died.

Luke 24:33-48

Did Jesus open the door and come in?

Jesus Goes Back to Heaven

ONE DAY while Jesus was talking with His disciples out on a hill, all of a sudden He began to go up into the air. Jesus went up into the clouds, and His friends will not see Him anymore. Do you know where He is going? He is going to heaven to live with God His Father. But Jesus will come back someday to take His friends to heaven. Are you one of Jesus' friends?

Acts 1:9-11

Will Jesus come back again?